80 Graded Studies
for **Violin**

BOOK ONE   Grades 1–5

Edited by Jessica O'Leary

Accompaniments for one study at each grade are available to download from fabermusic.com or by following the QR code above the study.

© 2017 by Faber Music Ltd
Bloomsbury House, 74–77 Great Russell Street, London WC1B 3DA

Music setting by MusicSet2000
Cover and page design by Susan Clarke

Printed in England by Caligraving Ltd
All rights reserved

ISBN10: 0-571-53977-7
EAN13: 978-0-571-53977-2

To buy Faber Music publications or to find out about the full range of titles available please contact your local music retailer or Faber Music sales enquiries:
Faber Music Ltd, Burnt Mill, Elizabeth Way, Harlow CM20 2HX
Tel: +44 (0) 1279 82 89 82   Fax: 44 (0) 1279 82 89 83
sales@fabermusic.com   fabermusicstore.com

Introduction

As string players, we understand how crucial setting up good posture, tuning and tone is from the very beginning. This collection of 50 studies will cover all the core techniques from the elementary level to Grade 5 and give an opportunity to secure technique one step at a time. It includes works by famous pedagogues such as Wohlfahrt, Schradieck and Kayser as well as folksongs, contemporary studies and some original compositions with one accompaniment available at each grade.

All musicians practise elements of technique separately from their music, but that does not mean there has to be no *music* in your technical practice. These studies have been selected with their musical qualities, as well as their technical demands, in mind. The dynamics, phrasing and articulation play an important role in telling the story of each study and I encourage you to exaggerate and vary these to help immerse you in each technique. Changing the bow speed, weight and sound point, for example, will bring a whole new life to a *crescendo* and exploring these subtleties of technique from the earliest levels of playing will pay dividends later on.

Each study has an optimum tempo mark but starting slowly and allowing time to focus on the core skills will make speeding up controlled and easy. Standing tall with relaxed arms and shoulders, feeling the pulse internally, feeling a balanced bow sitting on the string and holding the left thumb and all four fingers in a comfortable and relaxed position are key aspects of technique to think about before you even start playing. Paying special attention to these will allow the other technical demands at hand to develop freely and quickly.

You will find harmonics, to avoid gripping with the left thumb and highlight the need for a parallel and slighted tilted bow, shifting at early levels to remove that feeling of being 'fixed' and left-hand *pizzicato* and double stops to strengthen posture of the left hand. Feel free to use the studies in other positions, keys and strings to reinforce the ideas.

Many thanks to composer friends Richard Knight and Eric Crees for their stylish accompanied studies.

I hope you will enjoy hearing and feeling your skills develop on every single page!

Jessica O'Leary

1

parallel bows • 4th finger control

Andante (♩ = 104)

Henry Schradieck

2

varying bow length and weight • slurs on up- and down-bows

Gently (♩ = 120)

Wolfgang A. Mozart

3

changing finger patterns • slurs • 4th finger tuning

Steady (♩ = 100)

Folksong

4

slurs • rests • bow division in changing dynamics

Gently (♩ = 84)

Chinese folksong

5

varied rhythms • arm levels • double-stops

Firmly (♩ = 108)

Jessica O'Leary

6

3-note slurs • *legato* • singing tone

Accompaniment available

Flowing (♩. = 60)

Richard Knight

7

left-hand pizz. • harmonics • double-stops

Happily (♩ = 108)

Jessica O'Leary

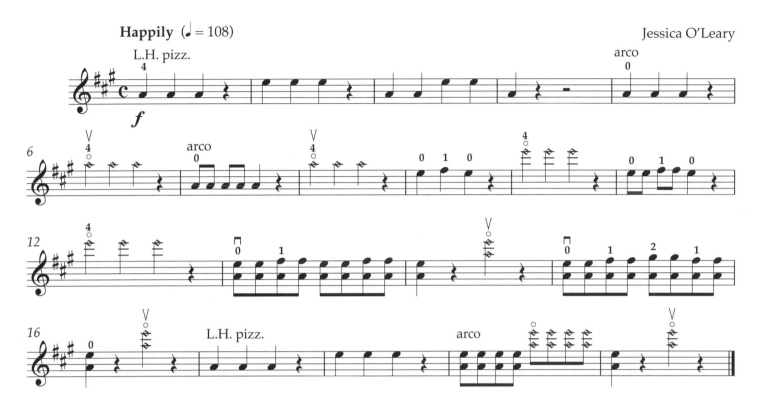

8

string crossings in slurs • changes of tempo

Dance (♩ = 80)

Richard Hofmann

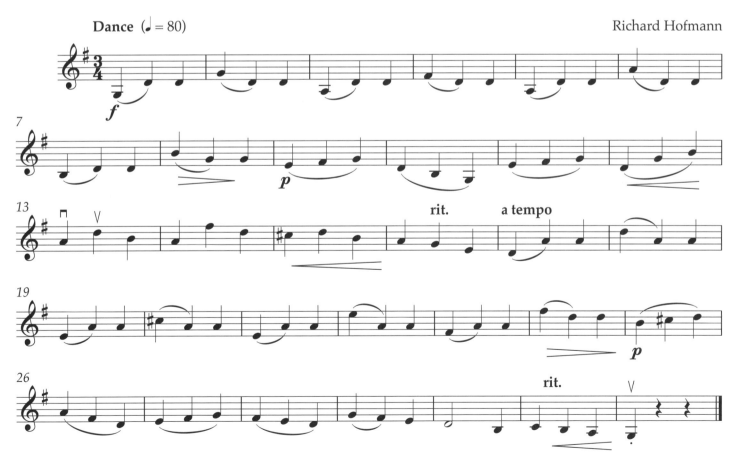

9

shaping with varied bow lengths • slurs

Allegro (♩ = 132)

Wolfgang A. Mozart

10

pizz. • double-stops • slurs across strings

Lively (♩ = 112)

Folksong

11

moving 2nd fingers • bow division in quavers and crotchets

Moderato (♩ = 100)

Joseph Haydn

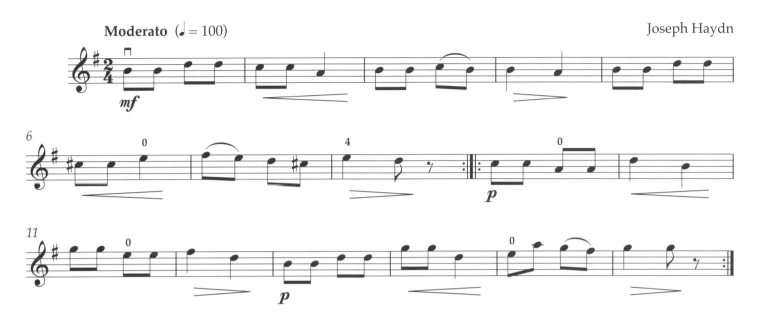

12

scales and broken chords • good hand shape

Feel in 2 (♩ = 104)

George F. Handel

13

independent fingers • clean string crossings

R. Steffani

14

2- and 3-note slurs • bow lifts • control on pause

Eric Crees

15

staccato bowing • *strong dynamic contrasts* • *slurs*

Carl Maria von Weber

16

dotted rhythms • *lifted up-bows*

Folksong

17

changing finger patterns • 4-note slurs • independent fingers

Joachim and Moser

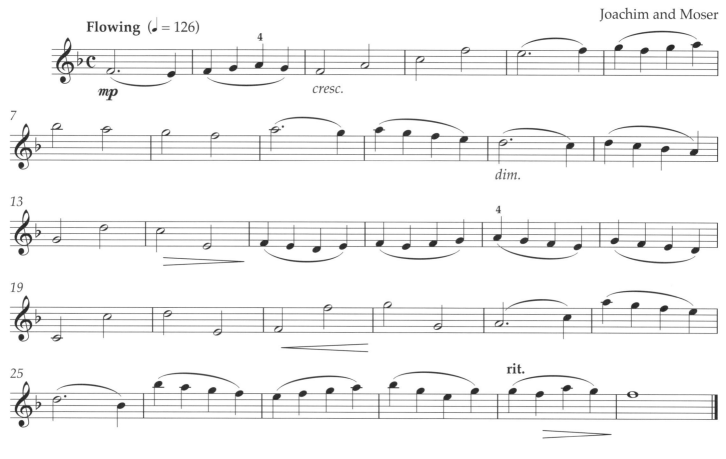

18

harmonics • left-hand pizz. • counting rests

Jessica O'Leary

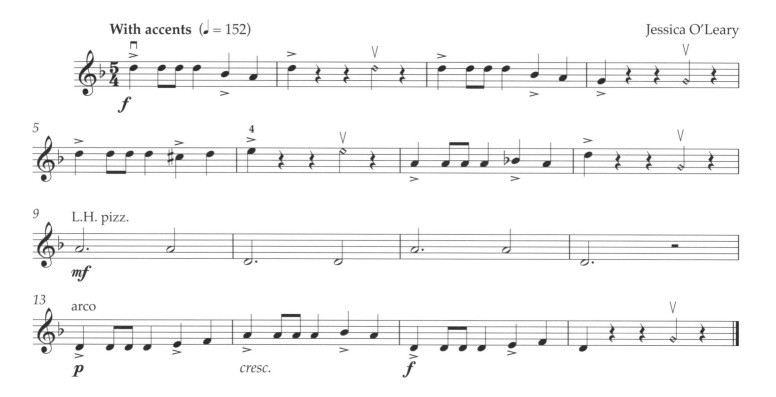

19

2nd position • close 3rd and 4th fingers • left-hand posture

Gently (♩ = 72)

Trad.

20

syncopations • pizz. • strong dynamic contrasts

Accompaniment available

Lively (♩ = 120)

Richard Knight

21

left-hand pizz. • shift to harmonic • hand position

Jessica O'Leary

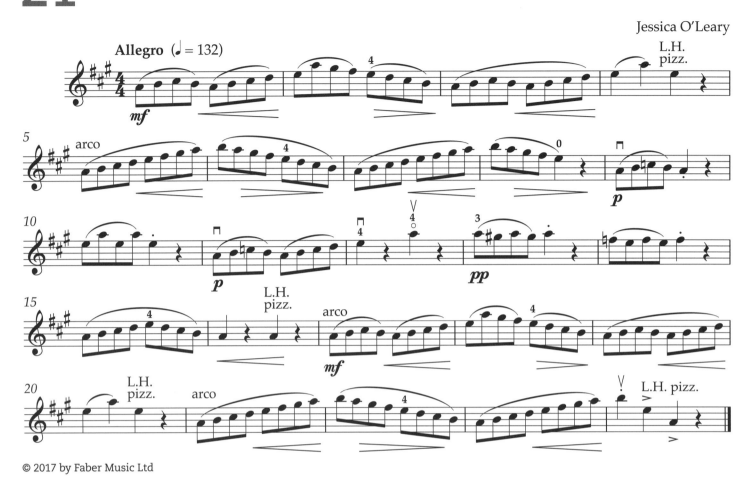

Allegro (♩ = 132)

22

rotating right arm • 1st finger back extension • varying bow length

Franz Wohlfahrt

Allegro moderato (♩ = 118)

23

independent left-hand fingers • use of mid-bow • clean string crossing

Richard Hofmann

Andante (♩ = 76)

24

double-stops • whole arm rotation • bow weight

Jessica O'Leary

Energetically (♩ = 92)

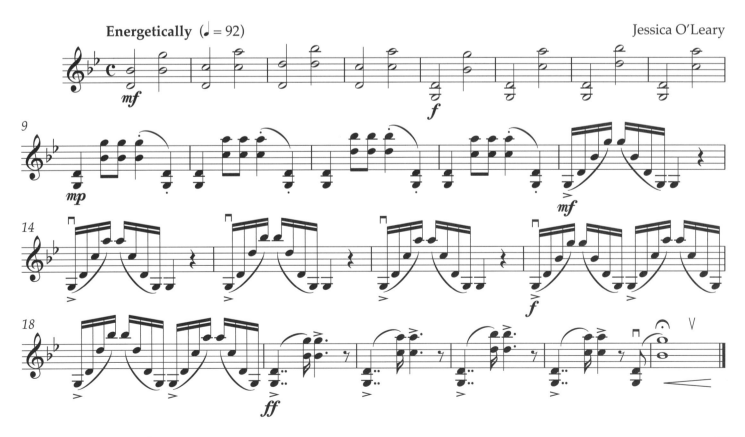

25

1st, 2nd and 3rd positions • shifting • floating bow

Gently (♩ = 88)

Antonín Dvořák

26

right-hand semiquaver finger movement at both ends of bow • *staccato*

Allegro (♩ = 96)

Friedrich Hermann

27

1st and 2nd positions • rotating right arm

Steady ($\quad$ = 90)

Hans Sitt

© 2017 by Faber Music Ltd

28

1st–3rd position slides • syncopation

Relaxed ($\quad$ = 100)

Jessica O'Leary

29

lifted up-bows • poise on *staccato* •
1st finger back extensions

Accompaniment available

Moderato (♩ = 72)

Johann Sebastian Bach

30

light 1st–3rd position shifts • harmonics • *vibrato*

Jessica O'Leary

Tenderly (♩. = 66)

31

chromatics • chords • slurs

Allegro moderato ($\quarternote$ = 108)

Friedrich Hermann

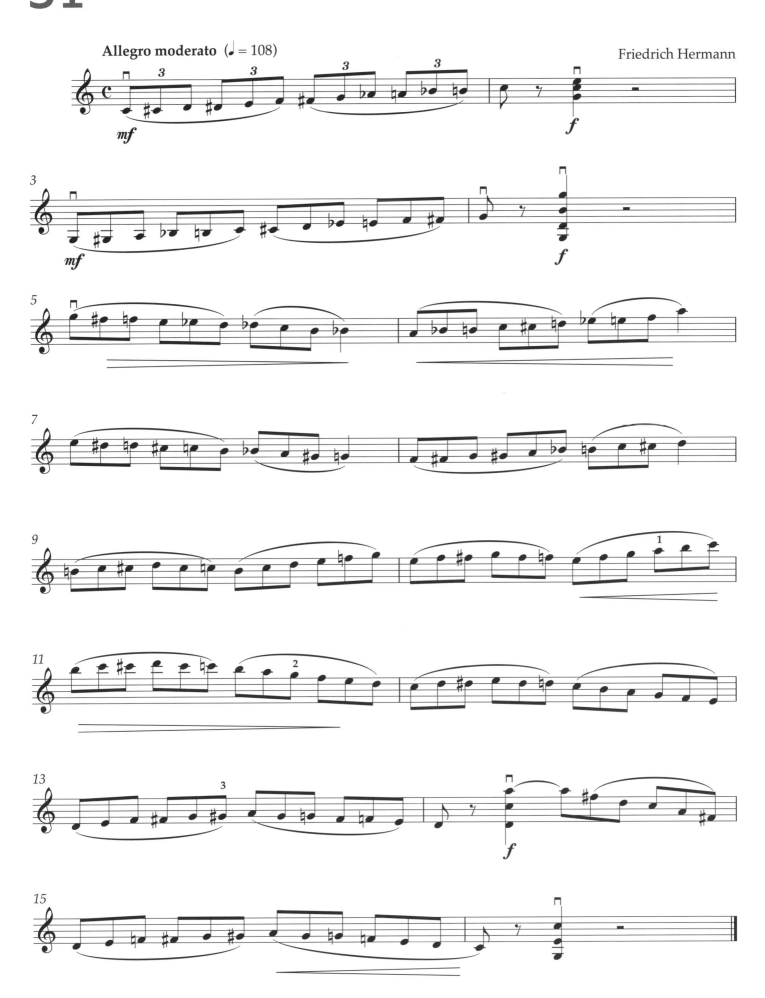

32 double-stops in *staccato* and slurs • 1st position

Hans Sitt

Moderato (♩ = 76)

33

1st, 2nd, 3rd and 5th positions • clear articulation • left-hand posture

Allegro moderato (♩ = 69)

Jacques F. Mazas

Tempo di marcia (♩ = 92)

Franz Wohlfahrt

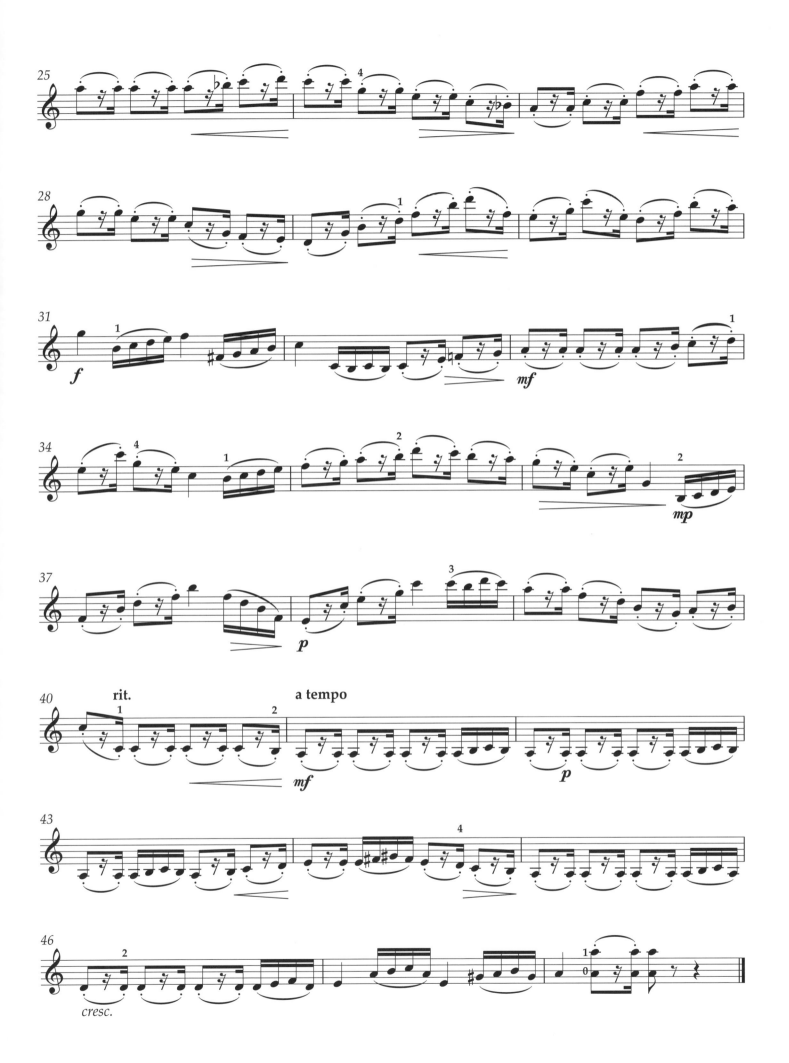

35

spiccato • back extensions • string crossing

Heinrich E. Kayser

36

mid-bow stroke on four strings • 4th finger • 1st and 3rd positions

Allegro (♩ = 76)

Arcangelo Corelli

mf leggiero

cresc.

dim.

_p_

cresc.

dim.

un poco rall.

_mf_   _p_

37

left-finger dexterity and stamina   •   1st–4th positions

Un poco allegro (♩ = 52)

Charles Auguste de Bériot

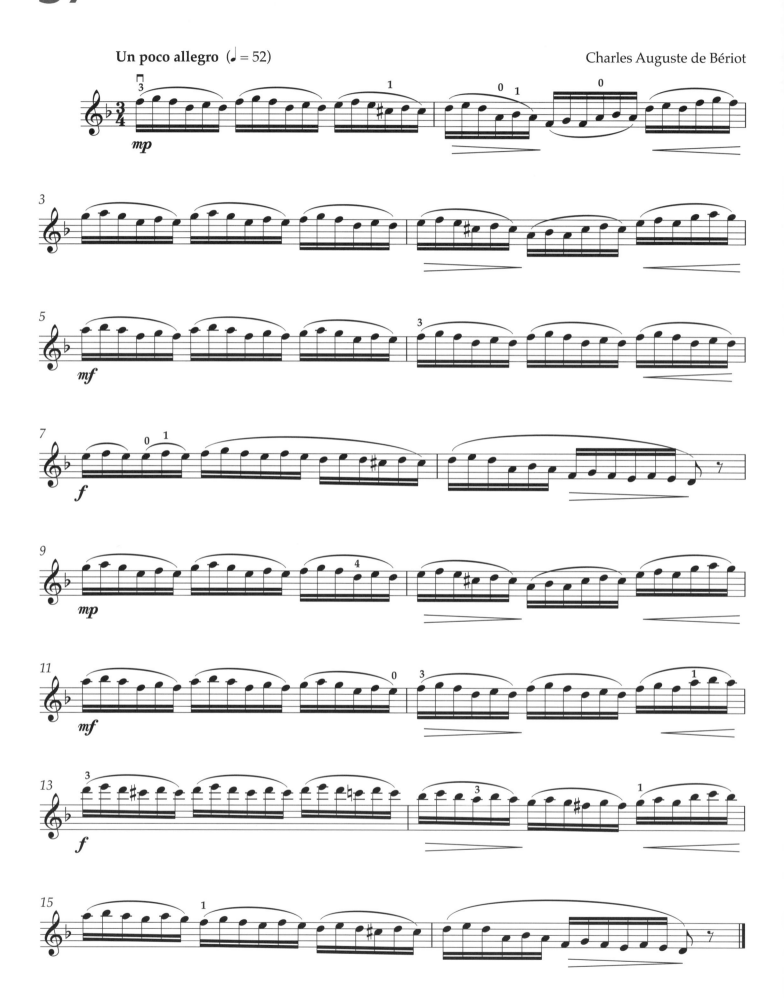

38

spiccato • 1st–3rd positions • repeated up-bows • syncopation

Allegretto ($\bullet$ = 60)

François-Joseph Gossec

39

broad *detaché* • bow division • controlled accents

Allegro moderato con fuoco (♩ = 76)

Richard Hofmann

40

slides • 1st and 3rd positions • chromatics

Relaxed and swung (♩ = 100)

Eric Crees

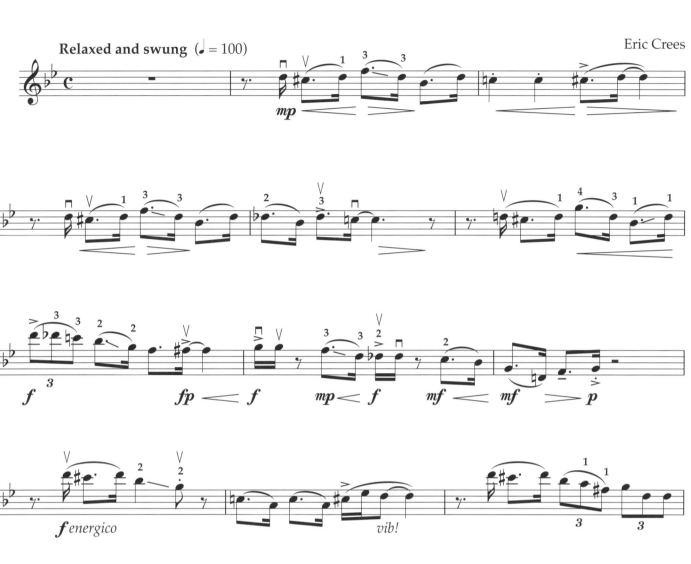

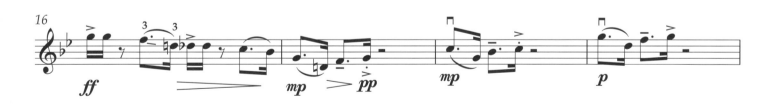

41

1st–4th position shifts • string crossing under slurs • rotation of both arms

Charles-Auguste de Bériot

42

chromatics • 1st and 3rd position • arpeggios under slurs

Allegro moderato (♩. = 44)

Franz Wohlfahrt

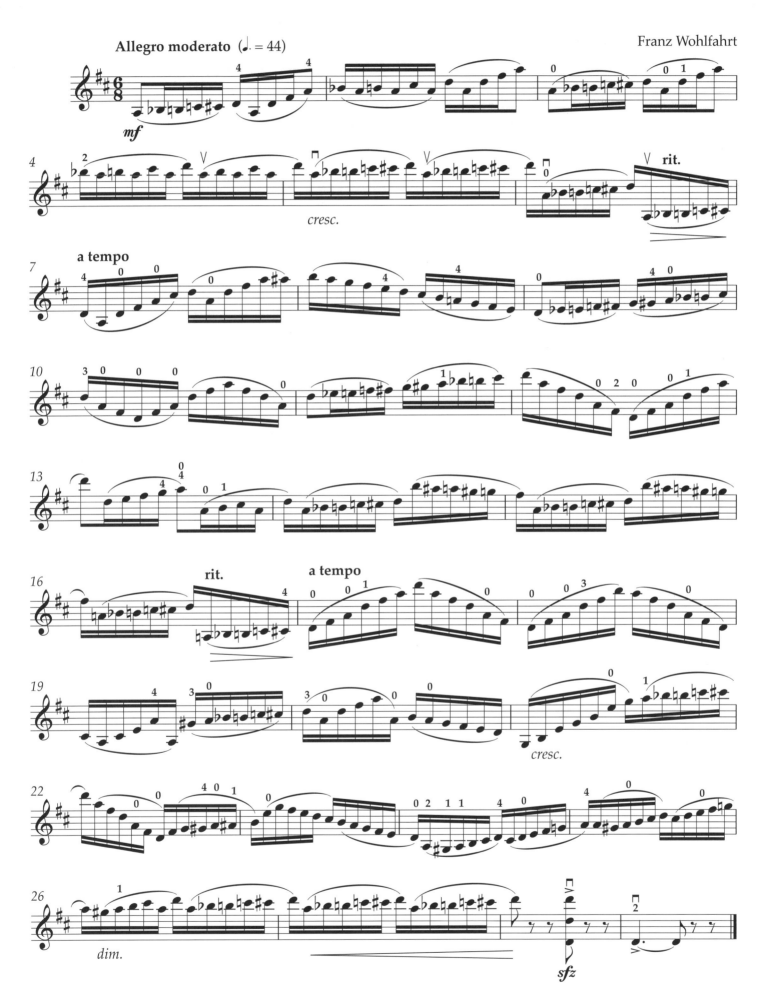

Ferdinand Ries

© 2017 by Faber Music Ltd

44

1st–4th position • shifts • bow management

Hans Sitt

45

1st–4th position • *vibrato* • *legato string crossing*

Charles Dancla

46

martelé stroke • clarity in string crossings

Jacques F. Mazas

Allegro non troppo (♩ = 82)

48

hooked bowing • right-arm rotation • quick shifts

Tema
Quasi Presto (♩ = 68)

Niccolò Paganini

Var. 2

Var. 7
a tempo

© 2017 by Faber Music Ltd

49

slides • 1st–7th positions • trills • pizz.

Richard Knight

Accompaniment available

50

double-stops • pizz. in both hands • chords

Heinrich E. Kayser